Dear Kathy,

I wanted to share this little treasure with you from our friend, Henri Nouwen --

I know that I can never be reminded too often that I am His beloved, and I want you to be reminded, too.

I love you and am grateful to be on our day-to-day journey together.

"Merry Christmas!", 2009

Alesia

Beloved

HENRI J. M. NOUWEN

Beloved

Henri Nouwen
in Conversation

with

Philip Roderick

WILLIAM B. EERDMANS PUBLISHING COMPANY

GRAND RAPIDS, MICHIGAN / CAMBRIDGE, U.K.

First published 2007 in the U.K.

with the kind permission of the Estate of Henri J. M. Nouwen

www.HenriNouwen.org

by the Canterbury Press Norwich

This edition published 2007 in the United States of America by

Wm. B. Eerdmans Publishing Co.

2140 Oak Industrial Drive N.E., Grand Rapids, Michigan 49505 /

P.O. Box 163, Cambridge CB3 9PU U.K.

Printed in the United Kingdom

12 11 10 09 08   7 6 5 4 3 2

ISBN 978-0-8028-6286-0

www.eerdmans.com

Contents

About Henri Nouwen

The internationally renowned priest and author, respected professor and beloved pastor Henri Nouwen wrote over 40 books on the spiritual life. He corresponded regularly in English, Dutch, German, French and Spanish with hundreds of friends and reached out to thousands through his Eucharistic celebrations, lectures and retreats. Since his death in 1996, ever increasing numbers of readers, writers, teachers and seekers have been guided by his literary legacy. Nouwen's books have sold over two million copies, published in over 22 languages.

Born in Nijkerk in Holland on 24 January 1932, Nouwen felt called to the priesthood at a very young age. He was ordained in 1957 as a diocesan priest and studied psychology at the Catholic University of Nijmegen. In 1964 he moved to the United States to study at the Menninger Clinic. He went on to teach at the University of Notre Dame, and the Divinity Schools of Yale and Harvard. For several months during the 1970s, Nouwen lived and worked with the Trappist monks in the Abbey of the Genesee, and in the early 1980s he lived with the poor in Peru. In 1985 he was called to join L'Arche in Trosly, France, the first of over 100 communities founded by Jean Vanier where people with developmental disabilities live with assistants. A year later Nouwen came to make his home at L'Arche Daybreak near Toronto, Canada. He died suddenly on 21 September 1996 in Holland and is buried in King City, Ontario.

Nouwen believed that what is most personal is most universal. He wrote, 'By giving words to these intimate experiences I can make my life available to others.' His spirit lives on in the work of the Henri Nouwen Society, Henri Nouwen Stichting, the Henri Nouwen Trust, the Henri J. M. Nouwen Archives and Research Collection, and in all who live the spiritual values of communion, community and ministry to which he dedicated his life.

Reproduced by permission of the Henri Nouwen Society.

Introduction

Henri Nouwen was an extraordinary twentieth-century exemplar on the spiritual journey. He was a delightful admixture of vulnerability and intention, of passionate intensity and colourful exuberance. His talks and writings have been beloved by two generations of seekers, saints and mentors.

This CD and book is the record of a treasured conversation. I hope that you as reader and listener will allow the insights gained to enrich your journey. Henri's wisdom forged through suffering and personal commitment shines clearly. By the grace of the Holy Spirit, may his perceptiveness gently guide and sustain your orientation towards life-affirming patterns and possibilities.

It was a delight for me to meet up with Henri at a retreat centre in England in the early summer of 1992. He was then living in the L'Arche community in Canada. I had known my resonance with his writings for some years and had found myself deeply drawn to Henri's directness of insight. This arose from his ever-deepening commitment to radical honesty and self-emptying on the way of Christ. I crossed some bridges and arranged to record a conversation when Henri was in the UK for a week or so.

It was not until the interview had been under way for about ten minutes that I became aware of the seating in the room. Henri was sitting in a rocking-chair. As he became impassioned at various points in the conversation, he would rock back and forth with some vigour. Seeking to maintain a balance in the sound input, I found myself rocking in a mirroring fashion, slightly desperately holding the microphone out in front of me as he and I rocked to and fro!

The interview, perhaps not unlike Henri's life, moved forward with a restless yet vibrant playfulness and profundity. Reminiscence danced with fresh awakenings, ancient tradition with contemporary perspective. Henri knew his call to be a disciple of Jesus, yet also his own fragility. He delighted in the dynamic of wisdom and embodied it with a distinctively soft angularity.

The call to a deepening and re-validation of silence and solitude as precursors of service had made itself heard and had left its mark on my own inner journey for some years. I knew I needed some further guidance in how better to incorporate in my active lifestyle the integral gifts of stillness, aloneness and active compassion as essential ingredients on the way of Christ. I was eager to benefit from Henri's wisdom on holding the creative tension of the opposites and my hope was amply rewarded.

[2]

This combination of stillness and action, this vocation to the paradox of finding being within doing is critical for health and discernment. As you will identify, the direction of the conversation highlights the truth that silence and solitude are precursors to service. This is evidenced in the Gospels and witnessed to by every generation of saints and mystics. Learning from this great tradition has inspired me to hold to this rationale of contemplation-in-action in the ministries that I have been privileged to establish and lead, most especially The Quiet Garden Movement (www.quietgarden.co.uk) and Contemplative Fire: creating a community of Christ at the edge (www.contemplativefire.org).

This is a profound time of challenge and invitation for each of us who sense in our hearts the opening of the contemplative way and the reinvigoration of faith, hope and love. It is a delight to invite you to share in the conversation between Henri and myself. My questions are printed in italics and Henri's responses are in Roman type. Do take it in small doses or in large chunks. May you be deeply blessed in your listening and reading and in all aspects of your own journey into God.

Philip Roderick
March 2007

The accompanying CD is arranged in tracks that correspond to the chapters of this book.

Henri Nouwen in Conversation

1. SOLITUDE

Henri, perhaps it could be argued that in a busy world, solitude and silence are key ingredients, but people find them difficult to come to terms with. Are they key to you and, if so, why are they so important?

First of all, solitude has something to do with being alone – *solus* means alone – and there are three words in English that are very important. One is aloneness – this is a very neutral term. There is loneliness, which is a negative term; loneliness is not a good thing. Then there's solitude. In many ways solitude is a way of dealing with your aloneness. You are alone – that's a reality – you are – there's nobody like you around. In a deep, deep way you are alone in the world. If a human being is alone, in the sense that his uniqueness excludes him from entrance into every part of another person, there is a kind of separateness. It's fascinating and important to know that we constantly struggle to overcome that separateness, particularly because we feel that our aloneness quickly becomes loneliness. This is probably one of the greatest sufferings of our time – that people are lonely.

In marriage, there is a lot of loneliness; in friendship, in intimate relationships, there's an enormous amount of loneliness, a sense of a yearning for communion. This is not satisfied, so enormous amounts of people suffer from loneliness – young people, older people. It is in the search arising from loneliness that people are looking for communion. They are looking for something to solve this pain. They do hundreds of things to solve it – one is entertainment, another is sexuality. Not all sexuality is to solve loneliness, but some people use sexuality that way. They use drugs as stimulation; they use travelling or visiting people; or they use being part of things, being busy. The more people do these different things – even work – the more they discover that they don't really find the response to their loneliness.

Augustine says, 'My heart is restless until it rests in you, O Lord'. You can say that much of what we are doing is to find some solution for our loneliness. On a very deep level, we know that if we want human beings or human structures to solve our loneliness, we can quickly become extremely demanding and obsessive. If you use your relationship to solve your loneliness, you

Augustine says, 'My heart is restless until it rests in you, O Lord'.

can quickly find yourself being very clinging and oppressive. This is why loneliness often leads to so much violence. You want somebody else to take that loneliness away and it doesn't work. You can see how quickly people's behaviour starts becoming violent – kissing is a loving behaviour, but it becomes biting before you know it. Listening becomes over-hearing, and looking tenderly becomes looking suspiciously. Precisely when they come out of loneliness, all these gentle things become violent things very quickly.

Solitude is essential if you want to live a life that is not destructive. If you want to accept your aloneness in a way that it becomes creative and not destructive, solitude is the way to embrace, to befriend your aloneness as a positive gift. It's like taking up the cross, because Jesus is saying, 'Befriend your pain, befriend your cross'. Your cross is your loneliness. If you embrace it and enter deeply into your loneliness it can be converted to solitude. It can be converted to an aloneness that becomes a source of life. Solitude is such an enormous discipline precisely because you want to embrace it and don't want to act out of your loneliness. It starts spinning, it starts becoming addictive. When you think for instance that drugs take your loneliness away, you want more drugs, and get hooked into it. Sexuality is the same. Work is

Solitude is essential if you want to live a life that is not destructive.

the same thing; you work, you want to talk to people, you want to be part of things, but, the more you do it, the more you want.

To break that cycle of addiction, you are called to embrace your loneliness. What does that mean in fact? Well, it means that somehow you claim your aloneness in a positive way as a gift, a gift where there is always pain involved, but a pain that you can live through. You trust – now that's the great jump – you trust as you embrace your aloneness, as you embrace your pain, you trust that it will get you in touch with the One who can really fulfil the deepest needs of your heart. Why? Because your heart is created by the One who alone can satisfy. The problem with God is that he's given us a heart that no human being can satisfy – only God can satisfy. So if you start embracing your loneliness, which means your broken-heartedness or your feeling of pain, you can only embrace it safely if somehow you trust that it will not lead you to despair. It will lead you to an in-touch-ness with the One who calls you to give all your heart, all your mind, all your soul to God and in that, give you the love that you want, give you the satisfaction you want. Solitude is a discipline in which you deal with your loneliness in such a way that it doesn't destroy you or others, but

You are created by a God who wants all your attention and who wants to give you all the love you need.

instead becomes a place to discover the truth of who you are. You are created by a God who wants all your attention and who wants to give you all the love you need.

2. TOO LITTLE TIME OR TOO MUCH

There are two categories of people – one, those for whom solitude is an involuntary context; in other words, those who are widowed, divorced, single, and who have no choice. Then there's another grouping of people for whom solitude is an immense luxury. They think, 'If only I had a bit of time to be on my own'. So, the first lot says, 'If only I had less time on my own. I need to be with people'. They perhaps need some ways to enable a creative use of their enforced solitude. The second group needs almost the reverse discipline to say, 'What is a realistic discipline of positive solitude? I want it, but I'm not sure how to deal with it'. How would you prescribe for those two different groups?

First of all, let me talk about those two groups. It's true that a lot of people say, 'I wish I had some time. I wish I could be more alone'. But you have to be aware that those who say that aren't necessarily the ones who can do something with it. In other words, busy, busy, busy people who have a lot to do, a lot of things to go to, a lot of people to meet, a lot of social things to do, start complaining. They start saying, 'I don't have much time for myself'; 'I wish I had more time for myself'; 'I wish I could be more alone'; 'I hunger'. It is a very mixed complaint, because their busyness is self-created. If you are critical about why you are so busy, you will quickly find out that you don't have to be.

There is absolutely no reason for most people to be as busy as they are. You want to earn more money than you need. You want to see more television than you need. You want to read more books than you need to read. You want to go to see more people. You want to keep in touch with too many friends. You want to travel too much. You can even be busy with looking for the meaning of solitude! If you're very critical of yourself, 'Why am I so busy, why do I want to write

> *There is absolutely no reason for most people to be as busy as they are.*

another book?' ask yourself, 'Well, why do I want to write another book? If that's what God wants me to do, what is busyness?'; 'If someone wants to talk to me, that could be interesting'. The discipline for people who say, 'I wish I had more solitude' – and this is a good desire – is that they have to unmask the illusion of their busyness. I shall have no time to pray whatsoever unless I radically say that prayer and solitude – being alone with God – is a priority. But my senses aren't saying that to me. I have to see somebody else or do something else or go somewhere else.

We live in a very rich culture – we are wealthy, we can travel, we can read, we have access to films and books and people. Solitude is a hard discipline, because we have the luxury of so many stimulations. If you help a person who is busy and who complains that there's not enough solitude, that basically is a call for radical conversion. Here we go to the depths of it; it is a question of spiritual identity. If you are busy, very busy, ask yourself, 'Why am I so busy?' Perhaps you want to prove something. Why are people so busy? Perhaps they want to have success in their life or they want to be popular or they want to have some influence. If you want to be successful, you have to do a lot of things; if you want to be popular, you have to meet a lot of people; if you want influence, you have to make a lot of connections. The problem is that your identity is hooked up with the busyness: 'I am what I do; I am what people say about me; I am what I have; I am what influence I have'. It is very real for me, it's real for everybody. If we say that we are the success of our work, it becomes true. As soon as you fail, you get depressed; as soon as people start talking negatively about you, or as soon as you feel that you have no influence whatsoever, you feel low.

Jesus had three temptations in the desert: to be relevant – turning stones into bread; to be popular – jumping from the tower and have angels catch him; to have power to possess all the land.† Jesus refused all that because he didn't have to prove to anybody that he was loveable. He was already the beloved. That's precisely what the Spirit revealed to him after he was baptised in the Jordan. The voice came and said, 'You are my beloved son, on you my favour rests'.†† That's who

---
† Matthew 4.1–11
†† Mark 1.11

you are; you are the beloved, so you don't have to be busy proving it. You don't have to run around. Immediately, that same Spirit who revealed to him that he was the beloved sent Him into the desert to be tested.

Solitude is listening to the voice who calls you the beloved. It is being alone with the one who says, 'You are my beloved, I want to be with you. Don't go running around, don't start to prove to everybody that you're beloved. You are already beloved'. That is what God says to us. Solitude is the place where we go in order to hear the truth about ourselves. It asks us to let go of the other ways of proving which are a lot more satisfying. The voice that calls us the beloved is not the voice that satisfies the senses. That's what the whole mystical life is about; it is beyond feelings and beyond thoughts. So that's one group.

> *Solitude is the place where we go in order to hear the truth about ourselves.*

The other group, the elderly, or those people who have involuntary solitude, who are lonely in the other way, those who have too much time on their hands – these are the groups that I am very interested in, simply in terms of spiritual life. We have a whole potential of saints, of people who can indeed take the reality of their lives and make what is involuntary voluntary. That's not such a crazy thing to say. I'm working with handicapped people. Nobody has any control over their mental handicap. Either you're mentally handicapped or not. The way you make an involuntary state voluntary, that's the biggest challenge. In other words, how do you embrace your reality and start making it God's way of calling you to share with the world a certain gift? For instance, you may welcome people who have no job but have enough money to have a little room and sit on their own. The church, the community of faith or friends are invited to help these people discover the source of their suffering as being the source of their gift. If they say, 'I have nothing to do', you could say very simply, 'Then you have time to pray'. That may not work right away, so you might want to go one step further: 'Why not discipline yourself to pray? I will just tell you for whom to pray, when to pray, what to read and when to read. You could call three or four people together who also have this time'. This is how we can do it.

The Church could come alive just from those whose involuntary solitude is converted. Interestingly enough, there are going to be more and more of these people who grow older and who have never been taught by the Church to live a mystical life. As soon as they are not relevant any more, not popular any more, have no power, they get bored stiff. There are people who are sixty to seventy years old who are bored stiff. The whole world is in pain: we need people to pray; we need people to think creatively; we need people to make phone calls; we need people for friendship; we need people to write cards; we need people to stay in touch with other people. There is so much loneliness, and many are sitting there complaining that they are forgotten by the world. They complain because interiorly they have no structures creatively to turn their solitude, their loneliness, into a gift for others and for the world. They are not even aware that they're still alive, not simply here to finish up their life. They are still alive because God has not finished with them; they have a mission in the world.

3. VOCATION

So, in practical terms, when a person sits in front of you as a sixty-year-old who is bored stiff, what structure would you suggest that would enable the mystical life to come alive for them?

Well, it depends what the situation of the person is. In my community, I have a lady of eighty-five years who I have invited to come to our Liturgy every day. She has a real presence and people love her. I invite people to join into a smaller unity of friends – invite people to come to a prayer group. Also we could say, 'Do you know two or three people who are in a situation like you, who could come together once a week for a few hours? You could have a Bible group or a prayer group, listen to a tape or watch a video about spiritual things'. As you grow in the Spirit, you then discover your vocation. But some people are so bitter and so resentful that whatever you do, they prefer to keep complaining than to be helped. There will be people who honestly ask the question, 'What do I do?' I am absolutely convinced that every human being who honestly asks God to give them a vocation will get it.

People who are elderly have an enormous vocation in life. It is good for young people to visit. It's good for elderly people to visit, but it's also good to be visited. Maybe you could make your house into a place where young people can meet some elderly people for a change. It's very important that the mystical life, which is the life of communion with God, is the life in which you hear a claim for yourself and your beloved-ness – that's what the mystical life is about. You claim that and live from that place, that's a choice. In the place where I live, I have two friends who don't call me up, I have two people who don't like me, and I have six people who don't give me enough to do, but I also have another reality in my life. What do I choose to live from?

I am absolutely convinced that every human being who honestly asks God to give them a vocation will get it.

Do I choose to live from the places where I constantly feel rejected, or do I choose to live from the place where I know I am the beloved of God? That's a choice, an inner choice, very hard to make. You may say something to me that I don't like and immediately I put all my energy into disliking it or defending myself. But I can also choose to say, 'Let it go, I am the beloved, he didn't understand it'. We don't have to make a big deal of it.

4. KNOWING OURSELVES BELOVED

Psychotherapists might say that a whole lot of people walk around, perhaps all of us do, with some feeling of lack of being the beloved, this stemming from our parenting and so on. Is the answer to that simply to say to oneself, 'Yes, I am the beloved', or is that too easy?

No, the answer is not to say to oneself, 'I am the beloved'; the answer is to claim our belovedness. There are anything between six and twenty ways of saying, 'I claim my belovedness'. For instance, there are all sorts of inner disciplines. Some questions leading to an inner discipline are: 'Do I keep choosing joy over sadness?' 'Do I keep choosing to speak a word of forgiveness instead of a word of revenge?' That is a very inner discipline. 'How do I spend my time, because there is a choice?' 'Do I read novels that don't get me anywhere, or watch TV that just makes me distracted?' Or, 'Do I choose to read certain books or watch certain programmes that really help me?' That's also a way of claiming my belovedness. 'Am I going to be a garbage can of the world, into which I allow any television programme and book to be thrown?' 'Do I have a big garbage can in my head?' 'Do I choose to say, "I am the beloved, I'm not going to listen to that stuff, not going to watch it"?'

Then there's the whole discipline of relationship. 'Who do I choose to be my friends?' 'Do I go to this woman knowing that I will be complained at for the rest of the afternoon, or I can go to someone who speaks to me about Jesus or speaks to me about helping?' Life offers constant choices, choices for the tools of my belovedness. That means discipline, and one of the disciplines is that which comes from community. Can I do it all by myself? Can I hold on to my belovedness when the whole world is trying to tell me I am not beloved and therefore have to pay money so that I can feel beloved? The world is seducing us to pay money, to make trips, to do things, to get involved, in order that I find myself to be worthwhile. How do I fight all these forces? Well, I need other people who say, 'You don't have to do these things, you are loved'. You need friends who physically touch you. There is a lot of need of physical embrace – kissing, hugging, holding, very normal healthy physical contact – enormous need for that, among the elderly, among men, among women, among children. There's an enormous need for affirmation, for people to say, 'What you said was really good and it really helped me'. There is enormous need for having phone calls that say, 'I have been thinking of you and been praying for you'. There is an enormous need for having people around.

Life offers constant choices, choices for the tools of my belovedness.

[19]

The Christian community is a community of people who remind each other who they truly are – the beloved of God. And everything around us is trying to tell me that it is not true. That is a big, big battle. That's what we call the spiritual battle. This is not just sweet things, it's the fight for your identity. Every time you choose, you make a little step, and these tiny little steps take place every second of your day. I can sit here and say, 'Well, you know, I wish you would leave and then I can do my thing', or, I can get into this discussion and say to myself, 'This is God asking us to be together'. Then we can be together and use the time as fruitfully as possible for God's love. That's the choice I have to make – an inner choice – and then I have to trust that something good will come out of it. But I can also not make the choice and waste my time and then I am frustrated for the rest of the day. The challenge is to have people aware, to empower people to choose and to know that they have a choice.

5. THE HEART

Linked in with the idea of the beloved is the heart. As to the heart in the Bible, we hear of Pharaoh's heart being hardened and Lydia's heart in the Acts being opened, so there is again a link with choice. We can go one of two ways; our heart can close in or open out. It's a fascinating concept, isn't it? Can you say a little bit about how you understand the heart?

Well, in the biblical understanding, heart is the centre of our being. It's not a muscle, but a symbol for the very centre of our being. Now the beautiful thing about the heart is that the heart is the place we are mostly ourselves. It's like the core of our being, it's the spiritual centre of our being. Solitude and silence, for instance, are ways to get to the heart, because the heart is the place where God speaks to us, where we hear the voice who calls us the beloved. This is precisely in the most intimate place. In the famous story, Elijah was standing in front of the cave. God was not in the storm, God was not in the fire and not in the earthquake, but God was in that soft little voice.[†] That soft little voice we have to hear, speaks

the heart is the place where God speaks to us, where we hear the voice who calls us the beloved

---

[†] 1 Kings 19

to the heart. Prayer and solitude are ways to listen to the voice that speaks in our heart, in the centre of our being. One of the most amazing things about that concept is that if you enter deeper and deeper into that place, you not only meet God, but you meet the whole world there.

If you give your whole heart and your whole mind and your whole strength to God, then you discover your neighbour there. 'Love God with all your heart, all your mind, all your soul, and your neighbour as yourself.'†† That means that in the total embrace of God's love, that is where you find many of us. If I go into my heart and meet God there, I always meet the world there. When God speaks in my heart, my heart becomes as wide as the world. It becomes like the marketplace of the world. A lot of people think about prayer or solitude as withdrawing from the world into a private space, but that's not at all the case. The contemplative life, this mystical life, shows that the deeper you enter into the solitude and the deeper you come into the heart, the more in the world you are. That's precisely the basis in the world. Therefore I've never personally believed in contemplation as filling up your batteries so you can go back into the world. I think of contemplation as precisely where you go into the world. Solitude and prayer bring you into a spiritual communion with the whole people.

†† See Mark 12.30–31

I don't know if you've ever seen one of these big wagon-wheels. They have a hub with all these spokes, but quite often we remain on the rim of the wheel. Prayer is to go to the hub. That's solitude, that's the heart. Prayer is going to your heart, but it's also going to the heart of the world and all the spokes get together right there. It is not that you lose contact, in fact you are more connected with people when you're in the heart than when you run around on the edges. Spiritually speaking, that is what intercessory prayer is all about. It is to enter into the heart of God and be there in communion not only with God, but also with humanity. My deepest conviction is that communion with God and solidarity with all of humanity always go together. You cannot live in communion with God without living in solidarity with people; it is essentially the same. That's why every mystic is an activist in that sense, because mystical people are not people who sit there and contemplate. Teresa of Avila ran around founding one monastery after another. John of the Cross was a very active person, and Thomas Merton, a very busy guy.

You cannot live in communion with God without living in solidarity with people; it is essentially the same.

With mystics and with mysticism, the point is that when you come to the heart of God, you touch God's communion with all people. You will know how you are being sent into the

[23]

world. You are sent into the world and that's what you have to do. I can sit here and say, 'Should I go to Somalia, or to Bosnia?' 'Should I go to Florida to help with the storm or whatever?' I have to sit here and stay here. Don't try running around, because it's very clear that I can't. This is my vocation. Then I have to ask, 'How does God call me to something new?' It might well be that that's not always the case. It might be that something happens in the world that I'm called to respond to in a new way. I have to, but it has to come from the heart, it has to come from God. Otherwise it becomes a set-up for burn-out, because I'm doing it in order to prove something to myself or to the world, or do good, or do something well. Then I am going to be bitter and disappointed.

6. PRAYER

Take the person who's been praying for a while and says, 'Well, this is all very well, but I've been having my quiet time for ten years or five years or three months or whatever. I'm not getting any sense of God speaking or any warmth. It's just that I'm doing it and I'm not getting any sense of being led. I want to experience more'. How do you respond to that?

I would say very radically that God does hear us. When somebody prays seriously, they understand that. Prayer is not spiritual gymnastics or heavy inner concentration exercises. The way I see it, prayer is first of all entering into communion with God, and God's people. People pray not just by sitting in a corner all by themselves, but pray in the sense of remaining constantly in communion with God and with other people – with those who would pray. Take Benedict or Francis, all those good people, they prayed, but before they knew it, they had a whole community going.

What about married people? The same thing; if married people are seriously considering the spiritual life, they start forming bonds with one another, they start listening to each other, start caring for each other. If somebody really wants to know what God wants them to do, I think God is so eager to have somebody ask that question, that he won't wait a second to respond. If you say to God, 'I will do anything you want me to do', as long as you are clear about it, you will get more clarity than you want! God is not necessarily always asking you difficult or profound things – to go on missions or to give all your money away – that seldom happens. God is usually saying, 'Why don't you do this little thing: just don't get so mad with your wife', or 'Maybe you should start reading a book'. It suddenly becomes clear to you, very clear, 'That this little thing I really should do'. It's amazing when you do one or two a day of these tiny little things. It starts carving a new place in your life and you find yourself – introspectively – having made a whole journey.

God is usually saying, 'Why don't you do this little thing . . .'

All great vocations take place very slowly. If you read their stories, Ignatius or St Francis, they weren't suddenly converted, they kept fighting and struggling for years and even when they had found it, they were still struggling like crazy. From a distance, most of these lives look a lot more harmonious than they really are. God doesn't leave you alone. If a person says to me, 'Well, I've been praying for so long and I've never had an experience of God', I say, 'Why don't you come with me, pray with me? Sit there with me and we'll read together, sing a song, and pray every day for ten minutes', or, 'Come to my community. You are much too alone. God doesn't want you to be alone, he wants you to be loved'. If people say, 'Well, I pray and I think', I say, 'You don't need to pray, you need a hug, that's what you need, and a good meal, instead of being so serious about your spiritual life'. It's a physical, incarnational thing.

Solitude and silence as such can be methods and strategies just as phoney as everything else. But they can point to a certain truth that we have a place where God wants to talk to us, and that we want to speak with God, to be with God. Let me give you an example: I don't have much time to pray in my community. There are such seriously handicapped people there. They can't talk, they can't walk, the only thing they want is that you hold them. Everybody's happy when I come for an hour to take over. I'm going to hold Adam in my arms for an hour, going to give him food. God gives me Adam to slow me down. I don't have time to sit in a church and do meditation, but Adam is there. Sometimes the nudge comes from different places. It's not always in solitude. It's not always in community. Community is essential for life, but there are millions of ways of realising community. Solitude is essential for life, but there are millions of ways to realise solitude. It's not all getting up at five in the morning

there are millions of ways to realise solitude. It's not all getting up at five in the morning and sitting in front of my icon for an hour.

and sitting in front of my icon for an hour. For some people that's the way, but for most people, that is not what they are called to, but they are still called to solitude.

7. SILENCE

Say a bit about silence, another major ingredient of Christian spirituality. Are we too distracted? We may have a certain degree of silence in our lives, but we're afraid, or we're too hectic. People often say, 'Well, I sit and try and be quiet but within seconds my mind is buzzing like a hive of bees.'

I wrote about these things in *The Way of the Heart*. I wrote about silence. This is a little Taoist story, a little saying of Chuang Tzu. It says, 'The purpose of a fish trap is to catch fish; when the fish are caught, the trap is forgotten. The purpose of a rabbit snare is to catch rabbits; when the rabbits are caught, the snare is forgotten. The purpose of the word is to convey ideas; when the ideas are grasped, the words are forgotten. Where can I find a man who has forgotten words? He is the one I would like to talk to'.

Now that's a funny story, but it's very, very true. In a way, words are there to communicate something, but at the same time what you want to communicate is also larger than words. That's even true in my conversation with you. I talk for an hour about solitude or silence and I still don't say it. I talk around it. Finally, once you catch the idea of solitude or silence, you don't need that many words about it any more. So, words are a way to silence.

I'm surrounded by words, and people have talked to me most of my life in lectures and talks and so on. I have talked to others most of my life, but beyond these words there is a reality that we have to dwell in. That reality is wordless because words divide things, spread them out. That's why it's so important that you know how to go beyond words. In my community, it's very important that words lead to silence, so that you can talk to someone for a while and then be silent with that person for a while. At a Trappist monastery – I was there twice for seven months – one of the things that I started to discover was that the silence there was one of the saving devices. As soon as these people, who always live together, would start talking, it would become the most boring place you can imagine. The silence kept them together in something larger than their words could express. On the other hand, silence also leads to words. If you are practising silence, it can be the physical silence of not speaking, but also an inner silence. If you practise silence a lot, your word becomes pregnant, becomes full. When people talk to you, sometimes it doesn't come from silence; it's rattling, it's noisy. Some people can say very few things, sometimes very simple things, and yet it's enough to make you understand things.

I remember I was visiting Mother Teresa in Rome. Everyone wanted to see her and I wanted to see her too. I went there as I had some problems. I had some personal struggles – quite a few actually – and I wanted to ask Mother

Teresa how to deal with that. I brought all my stuff to her. I talked for about fifteen minutes – on the whole she didn't have much more than about twenty. I just talked about all my problems. Then she looked at me and said, 'Well, Father, if you spend one hour a day in adoration of your Lord and never do anything that you know is wrong, you'll be fine'. I was stopped in my tracks, and I said, 'Well, I guess a lot of people like to talk to you'. Obviously she didn't say anything that I didn't know, but suddenly it hit me as so true and so coming from the right place that that little word was enough for me. It was more significant than talking to anybody else at

. . . if you spend one hour a day in adoration of your Lord and never do anything that you know is wrong, you'll be fine'. Mother Teresa

length. That is because somehow her words came out of silence. Also because somehow God made me ready to listen at that moment. Silence is a place that can give our words symbolic power. Most words are just words, more and more and more words. Silence is a place where words stop. More theologically, God is silence. Out of the silence God speaks the Word and the Word becomes flesh and the Word returns to silence. That's the whole mystery of the Trinity, the relationship between silence and words.

8. LIGHT IN THE DARKNESS

In all of these things there's a complementarity going on. Solitude is intimately linked with community and silence is intimately linked with word. There is a flowing between the two. But is that where our culture is? We're heading over the hill because we've lost that balance. We are in urgent mode now. Are we heading for a disastrous mode, would you say?

That's not how I think, maybe some people do. I was reading a book about the fourteenth century and I tell you things weren't easy then either. Think about the Black Death, the wars, the killing, the murders and so on. I don't want to talk about silence and solitude or community and the word as urgent necessities in that sense. I want to say that wherever God is in solitude and silence and words, there is prayer and community. These are essential for our lives and for the life that transcends the world. I think it's so important that there are always people who live solitude, live silence, live prayer and live community and who are in the midst of the world. They are little pointers to God.

The world lies in the power of the evil one; there's nothing new about that. We don't have to get panicky about the fact that there is so much evil. That's precisely what the world is all about; it's in the power of the evil one. St John said that whilst in the world, we live with the mystery that the world is in the power of the evil one. That is why Satan says to Jesus, 'You can have it all, it's mine anyhow'. Jesus doesn't say, 'That's not true'. He says, 'But I don't want it'. So the point is how, in a world that is evil, do we create places that allow us to get a glimpse of God's goodness, of God's love? I have a feeling that we need to turn everything upside down. We are always surprised by darkness. A certain darkness is brought about by evil. If you listen to the radio, or watch television every night, you see the news. You see that the world is in the power of the evil one. We keep telling people, 'Look what happens, isn't it terrible? Isn't it awful? Isn't it incredible?' We keep being surprised by evil, but we should be surprised by goodness.

in a world that is evil, do we create places that allow us to get a glimpse of God's goodness, of God's love?

Evil is nothing to be surprised by, that's the condition of things. Jesus said, 'Light came into the dark and the dark did not understand it'. Light came into the darkness, and Jesus said, 'I am the Lord of life, of truth'. You together have to be little reminders of that; little reminders, not in the sense that you are not evil, because Jesus calls us all evil, but we also are the beloved. It's not like saying, 'Here are good people, there are evil people'. It's much more like saying that people who live and listen to the gospel, who live according to the words of Jesus, are constantly calling themselves to faithfulness.

They can also invite others who look for the same, because nobody wants to be a victim of evil. There are ways in which you can de-victimise yourself.

9. HOPE

But isn't there a language of victory as well? The Bible acknowledges the power of the Prince of Darkness over this world, but it also acknowledges there is a victory.

That is what Jesus is all about. Jesus says, 'I have overcome the world. In the world you always will have trouble, but be of good cheer, I have overcome the world'. That is precisely what our hope is. That is why solitude, community and silence are all so significant, because we believe in principle that the powers of darkness have been overcome. That is to say that we don't have to be a victim of it; we can choose not to be a victim. That is what faith is about, to choose not to be a victim.

And that implies freedom, which is a radical freedom. If the Gospel says that we can choose to get out of this mess, I personally can choose. But are we meant to be modelling it on behalf of others too?

We all can choose. Every human being is free to choose, to say, 'Yes' or 'No'. It is not always black and white, because we say, 'Yes' and 'No' at the same time sometimes. I believe very deeply that the human heart constantly can make choices. Not just Christians, but anybody can make choices.

> I have to keep choosing . . . to say 'Yes', Yes', and 'Yes' yet again.

That's why Jesus says, 'When I was poor, you gave me something to eat', or, 'When I was naked, you clothed me'. People said, 'When did we see you poor?' He said, 'What you did for the least of mine you did for me'. We know that somewhere we have to choose. Whether we respond this way or that, we are faced with constant choice. We make a lot of mistakes. It's not like once and forever; we are constantly invited again to choose. I know it for myself. I have to keep choosing, to keep making choices, to say 'Yes' again, to say 'Yes' again, and to say 'Yes' yet again. It's not enough to say it once; you have to keep saying it.

You choose because somewhere you say to yourself, 'Although the world is in the power of the evil one, evil has been overcome. I don't have to become a victim'. That's where the illogical call of the gospel comes from: 'The last will be first', and 'He who loses his life will win it'. All these statements that seem to be so paradoxical break through the power of evil. They make you choose victory. Many people choose victory. Suppose you and I are in the same accident, and we both break our leg. The question is, 'How are you going to live with it?' That's the question. If you broke a leg, you can say, 'That's the end of my career', or I can say, 'This is the beginning of my vocation'. It's not what you live, but how you choose to live what you live. With this little group of people gathered together for Mass, if I describe everybody's life in the physio, you would see a lot of pain, a lot of struggle, a lot of difficulty. But somehow it's a very joyful community, because they've all chosen to live in a certain way, to live their pain in a certain way.

11. WORSHIP

So, finally, worship – that is obviously integral to your life and involved in all this process. What is worship doing?

That's a nice question. Worship, OK, let me say in the language we've been using, I have this image that God has been saying from all eternity, 'You are my beloved'. From all eternity, before we were born, we existed in the mind of God. God loved us before our fathers and mothers loved us. This whole issue is important, because in the world, my father, my mother, my brother, my sister and my teachers all love me, but they also wound me. No human being can only love us, they always wound us. We are wounded mostly by those who love us. We are wounded by the suffering of people in Somalia, but I am wounded by my mother who didn't love me well enough, or by my father who was so authoritarian, or by my teacher, or by my church.

The people who love me are always the ones who hurt me because they also have needs. God's love is a love that isn't wounding because it's eternal. God loves me from all eternity to all eternity. Life, this little bit of life – thirty, forty, fifty, sixty, seventy, eighty years, is not very long. It's just one little chance for us to say 'Yes' to them, 'We

God loves me from all eternity to all eternity.

love you too'. That's what life is about, and that chance to say 'Yes' is what time is about. *Kairos*, not *chronos*; *kairos*, the other Greek word for time, means opportunity to change your heart. There are as many opportunities to change your heart as there are events that you're part of. Everything is an opportunity to change your heart – a friend to visit, the mother who comes to visit, the museum, whatever, that's life. Looked upon from below, it's *chronos*; I have to survive, and I have to fight my way through it. Looked at from above, it is *kairos*; it's the opportunity to change your heart in everything you do.

In the beautiful story of the Galileans, Jesus asks about the Galileans whose blood Pilate mixed with the sacrifices: 'Were they any worse sinners than you are?' No, they were not, but unless you convert yourself, you will undergo the same fate. It is a very interesting tactic. In the news of the day, Jesus is asking whether the Galileans who were murdered by Pilate and whose blood was sprinkled on or mixed with that of the sacrifices, were any worse than we are. There was another news item that day of twelve people who were killed by the tower of Siloam. Jesus says, 'Were they any worse than you?' No, they weren't any worse than us, but we need to change.[†] In other words, all historical events are opportunities to change your heart; that's why they're here. All news items are

---

† Luke 13.1–5

meant for your heart to change. Why is there AIDS? There is AIDS so that you are converted, that's the spiritual answer. Why are there black people who are rising up for civil rights? So that whites can be converted. Why are the poor of Latin America poor? So that the rich can be converted. You know, that's the language from above.

Worship, to me, is constantly to say, 'Yes' to God's love; to say, 'Lord, I love you too, because you're beautiful and you are great. I love you too'. All of our life should be worship. Every occasion in our time should be an occasion to say, 'Yes, I love you too'. That signals a change of heart. The moments that we call worship, like Eucharist or Morning Prayer or whatever, are basically nothing else but moments in which we remind ourselves what our lives are about, moments in which we articulate in a particular way the essence of our existence.

Worship, to me, is constantly to say, 'Yes' to God's love

The problem for a lot of contemporary people could be put like this: 'Who is this you? Who is this God? Who is God?' Our culture, which is post-religious, although there is a sort of underbelly of resurgent religiousness, is saying, 'I can't relate to a you or a thou or to a God person to whom I'm meant to give thanks'. That's the existential problem.

I believe that there is something more than them, that there is someone to address and someone who addresses them.

If they could practise silence and solitude, would they realise that there is something other?

You name something of a contrast. You say that everybody wants solitude and at the same time you say everybody's asking, 'Who is this God?' The fact that everybody wants solitude is similar to saying that everybody wants to discover there is someone who speaks to them in their solitude. That's why I say it's an enormous act of faith to believe that if you start listening, you will hear something; or that if you enter into solitude, you will find intimacy; or that when you are silent you are not going to be dead silent, it'll be a lively silence. It is an act of faith that there is a God who loves us. I can't prove that to you, I can't even argue with that. I can only say that those who have entered with me into solitude, prayer, communion and into contemplative community, start loving each other, start really forgiving each other and start living. They discover that the grace to do that is a grace that transcends us; that there is someone else who sent us Jesus. They sense that God is not going to leave us.

God is not saying, 'I'm just staying up here'. In fact, God can take flesh; there is a person, there is a gospel, there is a story. I agree, most people have absolutely no sense of that, but I'm not surprised. We are so resistant to listen to that voice, because partially we want it, and in part, we don't. Partially we want somebody to love us, but we also don't want people or God to say things we don't want to hear. So there is as much desire for God as resistance against God. That's why God is called a jealous God. God wants all our attention and we are not sure we want to give it, so we keep privatising parts of ourselves. I am not surprised by that; it's not a moral judgement. That is just how the world is. Jesus makes that very, very clear. People at this time aren't interested in God either. They are interested in laws and ceremonies and things. I'm interested in somebody who really would break right through that – like Jesus – and didn't they put him on the cross?

> God wants all our attention and we are not sure we want to give it, so we keep privatising parts of ourselves.

13. 'LIVE LARGER'

What's happening now is that there are a lot of people who are not interested in anything of depth whatsoever. Some are interested in culture as depth, some are interested in spirituality and not religion, a sort of spirituality without religion, or perhaps a spirituality without God. But God may appear?

That's very true for people throughout the whole New Age movement. I don't know what to say – I love people, I love them if they believe in God or not. I'm not out to convert everybody, that's not my attitude. A lot of people contact me who have absolutely no sense of God, who I love deeply, who love me deeply. So I'm not saying that if you don't believe in God you're not a good person. It's just the opposite. Some of the best people are often people who have no formal religious interest, and a lot of religious people are very narrow-minded and extremely anxious. These lines are hard to draw, but I do believe that you continue to see people searching for the Spirit, searching for something that transcends the earth.

The quotidian – you know, the little daily work to be human – relates to our belief that the human spirit is given to us by God, and the human heart is given to us by God. We are called to 'live larger'. If our life is just made up of little things, it is no longer very satisfying. People are looking for a larger

People are looking for a larger beauty and a larger sense of life. That's the human spirit.

beauty and a larger sense of life. That's the human spirit. Whenever the human spirit is active, you see community, you see solitude, you see questions about silence, you see prayer, you see worship. Sometimes, the human spirit expresses itself in ways that are formally religious. Where a human spirit extinguishes – and that's what you see a lot – you get violence, you get very narcissistic behaviour, self-absorption, addiction, people getting totally lost, suicide, destruction and darkness. So there it is – if you look around.

14. PRAYER IN ACTION

Martha and Mary, the busy one and the contemplative one –
are we called to be both? Are there times to sit with Mary and
times to be attending busily? What was that story saying – as our
conversation draws to a close? There is an ambivalence about
the story, isn't there? Is Jesus rebuking Martha in an absolute
sense or is it just in a provisional sense that she has missed this
particular kairos?[†]

Martha and Mary were sisters, and both friends of Jesus. Martha serves Jesus; she does a lot of things for him. Mary irritates Martha a great deal, because she isn't helping out. Martha might also irritate Mary somewhat, because she's always running around and worrying about getting things done. For me, both people are, in a way, representing me or the human spirit. I'm very convinced of the importance of action. I'm very convinced of the significance of helping people, of doing things, of cleaning people and making meals and being hospitable – all the way to helping the poor in Somalia. This is very, very important: 'What you've done for the least of mine you've done for me'. But I also want to say that if our activity comes from our own insecurity about who we are, then it might not serve the Kingdom. Quickly our activity becomes the road to burn-out. Burn-out is basically

---

[†] Luke 10.38–42

activity without faith, wanting to prove something, wanting to show something. It ceases to be a free gift.

Jesus is saying very clearly that Mary had chosen the better part in the sense that if our activity doesn't come from being intimate with God, then it becomes a set-up for burn-out. On the other hand, I don't think Jesus is saying, 'Martha, stop serving me and come and sit with Mary', because then he doesn't get anything to eat! If you and I just sit around and are the kind of people who romanticise the spiritual life and make it all interior and praying and just sitting there having a wonderful time with Jesus and feeling good about things, we become part of this whole culture of interior swooning. But that is not spiritual life either. A lot of people are asking for the spiritual life and what they really want is to feel good about themselves. They want to have inner peace, this wonderful warm feeling. If God gives it to you, it's a great gift. If for a moment you find this enormous love of God embracing you, soak it up, it's wonderful, but don't count on it.

A lot of people are asking for the spiritual life and what they really want is to feel good about themselves.

For most people, their prayer life is dry, and as people get older, prayer becomes harder. Most older people have the hardest time to pray, and pray to have an interior life. It's not a question of having these inner harmonious feelings, though that is wonderful, and I wish I had more of them. But that is not what prayer is about, and Jesus is very clear about this. Jesus arose in the night to pray; at night he went up the mountain – and 'night' not just meaning the absence of the sun, it also means the absence of feelings and of thoughts. He was there and called out, 'My God, my God, why have you forsaken me?' This is the absence of the experience of God, but that doesn't mean you don't have to pray. That's what prayer is about.

Mary is called to faith and prayer, but not to make prayer some kind of romantic thing. She and we are called to more faith, to continue to listen to the voice of God, who calls us the beloved, to continue to be at the feet of Jesus. That's where my identity is rooted, that's who I am – I am the son of God, the brother of Jesus. That's who I am, and I want to keep reminding myself of that; to trust that out of that prayer, I will know to what action I am called. Jesus also says that it is not so much those who say, 'Lord, Lord' who will enter the Kingdom, but those who do the will of the Father. He says to Martha that it is not just those who run around being busy who will make it, but Mary has chosen the better part.

we are called to . . . continue to be at the feet of Jesus. That's where my identity is rooted, that's who I am

You might really like to look at Luke, when Jesus chooses the twelve Apostles. It says, 'At night he went up to the mountain to pray. In the morning he went down from the mountain and called his disciples together. In the afternoon he went out with them and preached the word of God and healed the sick'.† So, this is communion with God, community, ministry. That is the order of things – at night to pray, in the morning to form community and then with community to minister. Yet we turn it around; we want to do all sorts of things and if this doesn't work, we have other people help from community, and if that doesn't work we start praying. But that's not ordered from above. It's not a question of strategies or techniques or methods. God loves us and somehow we have to be very trusting. Sometimes we can pray and sometimes we don't pray. Sometimes there's some solitude, sometimes there isn't. Sometimes we catch community, sometimes we don't. But in the midst of that, God is among us. It is not that everybody should just shut up and have some solitude! Solitude and silence mean different things for different people at different times. They are not answers to the world's problems in a formal sense, only in a very deep spiritual sense.

Thank you very much.

---

† Luke 6.12–19

Questions and Invitations
for Reflection

Solitude

❀ What would be two or three ways in which you can befriend your aloneness as a positive gift?

Too Little Time or Too Much

❀ How deeply do you want to unmask the illusion of your busyness?

❀ Can you find a time each day to listen to the voice that calls you the beloved?

Vocation

❀ When do you choose to live from a place where you know you feel rejected?

❀ When do you choose to live from the place where you know you are the beloved of God?

Knowing Ourselves Beloved

❧ Identify some simple ways in which you can claim your belovedness, for example taking space to be with yourself.

❧ Discern ways in which you could encourage people you know on the path to remember that they also are the beloved of God.

The Heart

❧ Explore and journal how, when you enter into your heart, the centre of your being, you meet not only God, but the whole world there.

Prayer

❧ If prayer happens not only in solitude, but also in the company of others, with whom can you build and deepen a caring community?

Silence

❧ What are your ways of going beyond words? Begin to notice, when after a time of silence that you carve out for yourself, perhaps at the beginning of the day, that your words to others become more authentic.

Light in the Darkness

❁ Could you commit to create quiet places and spaces that give you and others the focus to savour the beauty behind the beauty, the mystery at the heart of life?

Hope

❁ For a week or longer, highlight ways and times in which you choose not so much to be a victim, but more to be a person of faith and hope.

Choosing Life

❁ How easy do you find it to keep on saying 'Yes!' to love and to life? Find three of four ways in which you can, on a daily basis, say 'Yes!' to love, learning and life.

Worship

❁ Experiment with your capacity to allow grace to change and open your heart, even in the midst of chaos, to give out thanks. Find the interior place where you can practise gratitude to God as Source, both for those who love and those who wound, knowing that often they will be the same person or group.

Desiring God, Resisting God

❖ Notice how you deal with the paradox that solitude is not privatisation. By entering into 'the cave of the heart', you may find that there is someone who speaks in the silence. There you may discover a new intimacy with the God who loves.

'Live Larger'

❖ Name for yourself and perhaps for a partner or friend, one or two examples of 'a larger beauty' and a 'larger sense of life' as you experience them.

Prayer in Action

❖ Pray, form community and then, with community, minister to others. How can your rhythm of life make way for these three ingredients of communion with God?